GHOST OF

GHOST OF

DIANA KHOI NGUYEN

OMNIDAWN PUBLISHING
OAKLAND, CALIFORNIA
2018

Cover photo: "Court," from the *I'm Not There* series by Pol Ubeda

Cover and interior set in Futura Std and Minion Pro

Cover and interior design by Gillian Olivia Blythe Hamel

Printed in the United States
by Books International, Dulles, Virginia
On Glatfelter Natures Natural B19 Antique
Acid Free Archival Quality FSC Certified Recycled Paper

Library of Congress Cataloging-in-Publication Data

Names: Nguyen, Diana Khoi, 1985- author.
Title: Ghost of / Diana Khoi Nguyen.
Description: Oakland, California : Omnidawn Publishing, 2018. | Includes
    bibliographical references.
Identifiers: LCCN 2017051224 | ISBN 9781632430526 (pbk. : acid-free paper)
Classification: LCC PS3614.G85 A6 2018 | DDC 811/.6--dc23
LC record available at https://lccn.loc.gov/2017051224

Published by Omnidawn Publishing, Oakland, California
www.omnidawn.com   (510) 237-5472   (800) 792-4957
10 9 8 7 6 5 4 3
ISBN: 978-1-63243-052-6

Thank you to the editors of the following journals and publications in which
these poems, though sometimes in earlier versions or under different titles,
originally appeared: *Adroit Journal*, "As from the Corpse, No Door"; *American
Poetry Review*, "Ghost Of"; *The Asian American Literary Journal*, "A Necessary
Death in Broad Daylight," "Family Ties," "A Woman May Not Be a Safe Place,"
and "Time Is Filled with Beginners"; *Bat City Review*, "A Bird in Chile, and
Elsewhere," "I Keep Getting Things Wrong," and "Reprise"; *Bennington Review*,
"An Empty House Is a Debt"; *Boston Review*, "Overture," "Gyotaku"; *Day One*,
"Grief Logic"; *Denver Quarterly*, "The Birdhouse in the Jungle"; *Drunk in a
Midnight Choir*, "Gyotaku"; *Gramma Daily*, "Triptych"; *The Iowa Review*, "The
Exodus" and "The Dictator"; *Lana Turner*, "Triptych"; *West Branch*, "Future Self."

Ghost Of is truly a brilliant book. Its textual innovations are immediately notable. They recall the work of Douglas Kearney or perhaps Tyehimba Jess's *Olio*. Here too, amazing poetry happens inside the visual dynamics. Note this "relineated" passage from an imaginative poem entitled "Triptych":

"There is nothing that is not music, the pouring of water from one receptacle into another a coat of bees draped over the sack of sugar caving in on itself"

"There is nothing that is not music" for this poet. Poetry is found in the gaps, silences and ruptures of history. Sometimes it is as if these poems address the reflection of a ghost in a mirror. Other times the poems here look off to a father's rooftop in Saigon. Or they look deeply into the interiors of family, a brother's silhouette in the doorway. The poem "Family Ties" asks "What good does it do, this resemblance to nothing we know of the dollhouse" and later, in "An Empty House Is a Debt": "There is a house in me. It is empty. I empty it. / Negative space: the only native emptiness there is." These poems mean to make a song of emptiness, the spaces we house. The poet begins one passage with "framing, an act of enclosing, of closing off yourself from your environment and all the unintended sounds" and concludes this passage with "we fill in what bewilders us to fill what." Thus the fragments and cutouts fill the void with music. The parts cut from the narrative become song while the remaining narrative becomes fragmented, half-remembered. The story told here reads like a kind of dream memoir. This is underscored in the series of altered photographs of the sort one might find in a family album. The images, like the poems, are intimate and unsettling; they are hazy specters of cultural and personal identity. This collection is steeped in the poetics of exile and elegy. In the title poem the poet writes, "Let me tell you a story about refugees. A mother and her dead son sit in the back seat of his car … Let me tell you a story about seat belts." Lyric fills in the holes in the stories. These poems sing to and for the ghosts of identity, history and culture; they sing like a ghost who looks from the window or waits by the door. *Ghost Of* is unforgettable.

Terrance Hayes,
Judge of the Omnidawn Open Poetry Book Contest

For my siblings, Denise and Oliver

Contents

A Bird in Chile, and Elsewhere

There is no ecologically safe way to mourn.
                                    Some plants have nectaries
            that keep secreting pollen even after the petals have gone.
Like a flower that grows only in the invisible
        the whole world of its body noiselessly shaking against the dust.

One

Around a pool of sorghum
thief ants lower their mouths and twitch in the feed

each animal growing by
accretion,   vote by
      vote,   the theory of seconds increasing
                  until the clock starts over—
the paycheck; DNA.

How long until the rice is ready?
How long has the rice been ready?

I feel my hair growing and know not what it means.

When we drove across train tracks
I threw my arms
across my brother's lap to absorb shock.

The question remains: Which of us had
the best life?
I can't be sure
but this will sting, I said
when I held my mother
and put my brother's hand
back beside his body.

The ants move closer
closer and closer.
The ants move into my camera and move on.
The ants move into my head
my mouth
I taste the ants I swallow the ants
a spider
could have woven around my mouth

like a room

a kiss

a woman still

burying herself

pulling off the world

like fly's wings:

the distance

between sugar stores   is grief.

I belong to a club that gets salt each month

from a sea I've never inhabited.

My mother scattered his ashes into the sea

and each night I draw a bath

with ashes from incense.   The real sea:

a sound with music and water.

In the future

is it possible to alter the half-lives of isotopes?

I cannot see the future

for myself or any of my doubles

but I see the days ahead of him.

Surely it cannot go on much longer, this desert oasis.

Surely it cannot go on much longer, this desert

in which the jet black

inkwell of my eye

spills, staining the ants who come to see.

mind
ful of
the setti
ing he co
unted off
the seconds
in his head a
s the solitary
bee struggles
to fly inside t
he walls of a
n empty hou
se, her siste
rs dead bel
ow her; no
wind, no r
ain; we st
ayed

framing, an act of enclosing, of closing off yourself from your environment and all the unintended sounds —car stereos, solitary bird in the tree, the male mouse alone in his cell who detects the trace of a female, pattering rain, neighbors upstairs spilling rice across the floors and slipping constantly, the drone of sister bees in the walls of your room lost for weeks, months, and each afternoon you wake to find a new bee on your windowsill, all wings still, and all the days unfold like this until you are not at the window, but the dead bees continue to come still, coming to a moment of our attention—framing, to get lost between the walls and open the mind to music; one must remove oneself or framing will remove you; you could not remove the bee that kept reappearing, (the sisters were unending); you could not remove the drone the hum inside your mind; you removed your mind—open the mind: all sounds are music; I am listening to a needle drop, I am listening to a needle drop, I am listening to a needle drop, I am listening to a needle drop, I am listening to a needle drop, I am listening to a needle drop, I am listening to a needle drop, I am listening to a needle drop, I am list

listening to a needle drop, I am list
needles I have always dropped th
hand of my mind my hands encl
amplified cactus of this palm of
different; let me not be the on
unintended sounds and all, let m
cactus begging for some new ap
attend to you listening in a mom
let me blur these boundaries betw
to all that drops—please—be no
resistance: our human ears have vulne

ening to—I am dropping all the needles I keep on dropping the
e needles the needles are stacked in my palm in the palm of my
ose the environment of the needles, what can you hear in the
mine? pay attention: each time the thrums of a dishwasher are
ly listener wishing that the music could go on a little longer,
e not be the only, let me not be let me not—this stupid amplified
proach to framing, to listening to unintended unattended I will
ent of attention to life my mind is open to the fact—let me beg,
een life and soundlessness, I will do all the exercises, I will listen
t art but life, be life, please be—here, a simple explanation for
rability to unfamiliar sounds; when you hear these sounds and feel

trapped, you must remove yourself from what surrounds you: these sounds, these sounds we have vulnerability to unfamiliar—remove yourself from frames remove the frame, remove the do not panic, do not panic is the simplest explanation the simplest resistance to music; do not simply resist, resist; we who are free to move around who are free, bewilder, we bewilder what we fill in what bewilders us to fill in what

I Keep Getting Things Wrong

After Mark Levine

1

                                        My father, just
out of his teens, stands on the rooftop
of the embassy in Saigon, his birthplace.
He gives his hand to his mother,
and all around them, a thousand hands reach up

not to wave. None of his siblings died.
Their bodies like a fine chain balled tight
in a fist. They made it out alive.
Why is he looking at me like this?

2

This is the idea of a house my father built
in Southern California. These two circle windows
and bamboo on all sides. He brought a jungle here,
complete with French doors.
These are the tiles from his mother's house, cool
against my cheek. I talk to him in one tongue,
he answers from the morgue.

3

Let's get on with it.
When I return to that house, I eat the food
left out for my dead brother. I don't waste much.
I slide open and close his closet, untangle

the window blinds. The bees are quiet in the
walls, now, their colonies dying off.
His shoes on my father's feet are the only moving thing
in sight.

4

On their flight to America,
the choice for lunch was rice or pasta, but when
the meal cart reached them, there was only pasta.
My father smiled at the flight attendant and asked,
Why didn't you reap enough rice?

5

The certificates we use to be certain of each other:
ID cards, contracts, permits, deeds,
fishing licenses, driving licenses, car titles, carry permits,
registrations, income statements, IOUs, testimonials,
certificates of birth, custody, and death, letters of consent.
Do I have permission to approach
a drowning man from behind?

6

I dreamed last night, my mother says,
that you were in danger and your brother was young still,
though you were the same
as you are now.
He was looking for me and I was looking for you.

7

I sit at my desk, typing and deleting
words.
Twice I dreamed I fucked my brother.
I keep trying to wake up. I keep getting things wrong.
I'm ready to feel better.

A Necessary Death in Broad Daylight

Alone in my seat of the roller coaster I seemed to be sitting in a church

The dead cannot distinguish

One female monkey with the resigned look of love at another engaged in
  breast-feeding

Even the lion licked the smooth head of the lioness

I must not be consoled

Suppose the person in me is a better mother than the author of a book
  I wrote

You reappear in a world which sees no danger in being nude, digging in the
  earth for black water, finding passage in hard soil because you no longer
  need to find yourself

A successful suicide, that's the phrase, is when the mother requests of her
  surviving daughters that they suppress joy over their lunches just before
  she removes her dead son's slippers from my feet, replacing them with
  others

Because, despite everything, you hadn't lost your hunger, eh?

Where I was young, where I was treated like a boy, where I was intelligent

He was alone in containing his violence

Is it not useless to pursue, for its own sake, the urgency of a previous day?

I loathe it—the likeness of a brother living in the likeness of a body, with lips
  and hands and eyes that keep nothing in, nothing out

I would give you my other face to touch

I love them—the likeness of a woman, in her arms the likeness of a child

Once more I begin to move in the direction of the animals

uncontained even
water abandons i
tself; there is mys
tery inside migra
tion, the elver s
wimming up a
head, out of th
e photograph;
eels who ride a
top each othe
r do not have
to see each o
ther face to
face; of the
road, it doe
s not mov
e, it is eve
rywhere
it has a
a story,
I am i
n it, y
ou a
re i
n i
t

uncontained even
water abandons i
tself, there is mys
tery inside migra
tion, the elver's
winning up a
head, out of th
e photograph;
eels who ride a
top each othe
r do not have
to see each o
ther face to
face; of the
road, it doe
s not mov
e, it is eve
rywhere
if has a
a story,
I am i 'uncontained even
n it, y water abandons i
ou a tself, there is mys
re i tery inside migra
n i tion, the elver's
t winning up a
head, out of th
e photograph;
eels who ride a
top each othe
r do not have
to see each o
ther face to
face; of the
road, it doe
s not mov
e, it is eve
rywhere
if has a
a story,
I am i
n it, y
ou a
re i
n i
t

27

As from the Corpse, No Door

Pale girl, fat carcass; boy uncut, unhooved.
The combination of girl and boy
in flowering desert. Girl and boy in flood,
brackish water. For the sake of children. Her brain
like cauliflower, cheesecake in dark rooms;
girl and boy: conscience between two mothers.
The upper half of body, the lower depth of honey,
rough beast, dark brass—burnt tokens from home,
remnants, chrysanthemums in a gale. Their olio of limbs.
Here then, new habitat: his forehead
in early sunlight where cold scarlet
and opaline mind, her cilia her sinew, mole underfoot.
Here then, her false-thorned earrings and sycamore skins,
wind white with petals wild from a week alone.
Alone, undone—like a father and a feather whose forecast:
breath, oil, fossil. Pharmakon: a cure as well as a poison.
In open grave, her hands deep in the pockets of.
The voice of a crane.

Gyotaku

sound itself
can be a form of v
iolence escapable only
in death it passes through
walls it rushes in it pierces
but does not touch—a victi
m bears no marks on his bod
y, the body moved by sound,
moved to leave it leaves no tr
ace; there are two sisters, wh
o are the two sisters—null
at the intersection of his
music and violence, it
saturates a space, *a
udire, obaudire,*
stay

Gradually a girl's innocence itself becomes her major crime

A doe and her two fawns bent low in the sumac along the bank of a highway,
    the pinched peach of their ears twitching in the heat

Into the disordered evening my brother cut out only his face from every
    photograph in the hall, carefully slipping each frame back into position

What good does it do?

Decades of no faces other than our own chipping faces

What good does it do, this resemblance to nothing we know of the dollhouse

New parents watch their newborn resting in a sunny patch of an empty
    room, the newborn making sense of its container—

And from the road a deer ripened in death and a tuft of fur—or dandelion—
    tumbled along, gently circled, driftwood, shaking loose, gathered,
    dissolving into the mouths of jewelweed nearby

Earth is rife with iron and blood is rich in stardust

Immediately I spotted one hoof print, then nothing, as if this was where she
    dragged herself out of the body

Strips of tire torn from their orbit

Is it right then, that we are left to hurtle alone

The Exodus

Saigon to Los Angeles, 1975-2015

For a long time, it didn't seem
        possible. Then the whispering
grew louder, the blur and hum of synchronous movements,
                as in a murmuration—
leaderless, with the shades drawn

        A poet burning his life's work, a mother
measuring out small bottles
        of poison

As my grandfather and his sons were ushered through the droves,
        remorse rose up in him,
tear gas bowling over and over and over

Then
        everyone became equals,
each one disappearing in the shadow of another

Touch as a bird rarely seen unless believed in,
wretched.
A youth points a toy gun at her chin, stupid
girlish pleasure rising for a moment

Still, every living body finds a routine
no matter its damage.
Two minutes after I was born
I had already made my first evacuation

Years later when I found myself in Saigon
I bought a lighter at the war market. Etched on one side
was a nude woman
reclined with her legs spread, an owl
at her sex, one wing in,
the other wing out, two owls standing by

Why should we mourn?
Isn't this the history we want
one in which we survive?

After many days at sea, my mother's guised boat
found rescue. A young man collapsed and died
      beside her, the journey's end too much to bear

Before my brother was born, all four of us
           slept beside one another in one bed.
     In an effort to resist memory,
my mother asked me to shake her awake

           The night before the monks came
to usher my brother out of the realm of the living,
     we gathered on the same bed, sifting through photos
and stories of him.
        At the funeral, his hand was warm
     where my mother would not let go

Maybe you'd forget
     why you were here, that you
didn't belong,
     that just because it was like life,
        didn't mean it could be life,
that you could come back to life
           but not return to living.
And if you bypassed a war, a war
wouldn't bypass you

with e
yes close
d he waits
for his bo
dy to do
the sam
e, a fistful of g
rains, rice let go fr
om the hand of a cy
mbalist; first the rains
torm then trio of cric
kets, a stream then a tr
ickle like someone who
has the hands of a mo
ther or father to gui
de him but the hou
se is empty, he is e
mptying out ever
y hour, all hours
before his death h
e is dangerously cl
ose to living, his bo
dy is warm his mind
cool; what are the tr
icks for warming; he
no longer feels the w
atch against his wrist
he no longer feels a
wrist he no longer

what may exist between appearance and disappearance, between sound and silence, as something that is nearly nothing—slow music, quiet music, spare music—of sound and form I fell asleep tonight after feeding us both it was hard to think of you cold it was hard to think you think it was hard to

think of you it was h

istling teeth, it has s

or everyone not eve

everyone is there

ng along the l

point depart

vanishing, n

duration to m

first then mys

space we occu

dream momen

e in the room

and back did

across the y

keeps me

ard to think; while I slept soundful the wind howled and whet its wh

ound but no form, what has a form but no sound? there is no sound f

ryone has a sound there is no sound for there is no sound there for

anyone between the sound and the silence, some solitary figure ambli

oop, no sound, no sound in which the performer is silent, he is a

ing, no sound no sound overtaking sound to the verge of

o sound, not one, no one silhouetted against the empty scores no

ark but still a space to occupy, an occupation; tonight I fed you

elf then fell asleep; we have departed from the cage, that is not a

py; a sister who is dreaming becomes a sister in another sister's

tarily forgetting that music is playing—something startled me, a voic

I thought was empty—did you jump over, did you jump back, over,

you jump did you jump back did you; over here I stretch the replay

ear, and longer, it keeps me alive it keeps me alive it keeps alive it

alive it keeps me alive it keeps me alive it keeps me alive it keeps

Two

The Birdhouse in the Jungle

The sky black with swans

casts the shadow of a hunter

over one flecked egg flushed from bramble.

Nature makes mistakes:

my siblings and I playing orphan

in the wilds we built with plastic.

What we witnessed of the world was a cloak

cut, sewn,
then fashioned into tinier envies.

In the unkennelled cold,

a bird's song

splatters against moist leaves

its lyric out of sync
with melody.

There is nothin
g that is not mu
sic, the pouring
of water from
one receptacle
into another, a
coat of bees d
raped over the
sack of sugar
caving in on
itself: inside
the house f
ull of teeth
he remem
bers what
a hand is,
but not
its nam
e, what
is its n
ame?
what
na
m
e

your body: it caught fire: how glad you we   re to
take it off, you took yourself off, you took y   oursel
f out, why did you take off, so we could tak   e you to
the water? two are the ways of going: looki   ng forwa
rd, looking back; the fog rolls in, folds us i   n, folds o
n in it is not my choice, it is not my choice   , it is not
my choice, it is not my choice, it is not my   —why here
you are, your hand, though we slipped you   into water,
here is the hand not cut out, the hand inta   ct, see it not
crumble like old bread—but where is your   face, I cannot
see your face; here is mine, water all over it   , sometimes th
at is better, you can take a brother to water   you can rage ag
ainst each other—what do the tides do? the   y go there and b
ack, there and back, there and unless it is u   nused, it is folded
into life unfolding life; it is not my choice, b   ut it is mine none
theless: I feel so dry I feel myself kindling I   want to build a b
ridge, I want to know its breaking point: ben   d forward, bend ba
ck, bend forward, bend back: can you reme   mber, can you send
someone back? end, end someone today, toda   y, you said, today we
can be less, we can be can we be can we rage against each other can
we rage with each other can we open the door can we cut each other
down can we cut the door out can we cut each other can we cut it
out; cut it out: why here I am, water on my face; I jumped into the
water, opened up my mouth: you swept and wept within me;
sometimes it is better, within, without, without this love running
out; it runs out it runs out of air it runs out of it it runs it runs out of

If you swim against the fish, your legs will grow longer.
If you swim with the fish, every bowl of water will tremble in your hands.
If the fish swim across your path, hang your head in imitation of a child
    hiding her face.
For there is no calm in life, not even underwater.
If there is a calm, it can be found after death, if something comes after it.
If swimming comes after death, you are not alive.
If you swim, you aren't swimming, you're unafraid in the ocean.
If you are unafraid, beware.
If you fear, it is yourself you fear.
For there's no one else around.
If there's no one else around, read out loud, just to hear a voice.
If you are underwater, be careful, the reef is under threat.
For others keep on living, or try to.
For those who try to live, there are those who won't.
If this doesn't end the world, the world will end after it.
If your brother dies, you will see your brother.
If your brother is killed, you will see your brother.
If your brother killed himself, you will see your brother.
If your brother killed your brother, you were a brother.
For the brother is a subverter of the sister.
If the brother is a subverter of the sister, the sister is a subverter of the
    brother.
If the brother is alive.
Each day I want my hair short. And the next day, the opposite.
Each day I want my hair long, and the next day, the opposite.
Each day is the next day, and its opposite.
That which is the identical on land is fraternal underwater.
That which has happened, cannot happen again.
If it cannot happen again, it is nothing.
When I am nothing, I am going to miss the groceries here.

ran
thru the
ribbon o
f his life e
ely eellike; b
orn and not b
orne the eel re
turns upstrea
m up dam wa
lls waterfalls
winding, win
chless, she f
ails her vow
to defeat d
eath so cel
ls divide li
ve divi
de

elv
er elve
r oliver
elver elve
r oliver oliv
er elver olive
r oliver oliver
elver elver elv
er elver oliver
elver oliver el
ver elver oliv
er elver olive
r oliver oliv
er ver ver e
lver oliver
ver lver ve
r o ever liv
e ver

elv
er elve
r oliver
elver elve
r oliver oliv
er elver oliver
elver elver oliver
elver oliver el
ver elver oliv
er elver olive
r oliver oliv
r ver elver ve
elver oliver
r oliver

ran
thru the
ribbon o
f his life e
ely eellike; b
orn and not b
orne the eel re
turns upstrea
m up dam wa
lls waterfalls
winding, winchless, she f
ails her vow
to defeat d
eath so cel

ran
thru the
ribbon o
f his life e
ely eellike; b
orn and not b
orne the eel re
turns upstrea
m up dam wa
lls waterfalls winding, win

elv
er elve
r oliver
elver elve
r oliver oliv
er elver oliver
elver elver oliver
elver oliver el
ver elver oliv
er elver olive
r oliver oliv
er ver ver e
lver lver oliver
lver lver ve
r o ever liv
e ver

elv
er elve
r oliver
elver elve
r oliver oliv
er elver oliver
elver elver oliver
elver oliver el
ver elver oliv
er elver olive
r oliver oliv
er ver ver e
lver lver oliver
lver lver ve
r o ever liv
e ver

elv
er elve
r oliver
elver elve
r oliver oliv
er elver oliver
elver elver oliver
elver oliver el
ver elver oliv
er oliver oliver
r
ver ver ver e
lver lver oliver
lver lver ve
r o ever liv
e ever

47

A Woman May Not Be a Safe Place

Melzack isolated young dogs from birth, protecting them from any painful
stimuli, until he himself began exposing them to burns, to pricks—the
dogs didn't understand the source of these sensations and were
surprisingly mute, struggling to figure out how to protect themselves
from further attack

A god let my mother suffer in Vietnam, now we go on suffering after her

She shot a man, one that she knew, that was during the War, so there could
have been others

A lover once pushed me into a ditch so he could help me up again—*I was
curious if you would cry*—

The mother met the father out West, after they had rejected adopting names
for themselves like Sharon or Sam, after they'd heard in church (the only
time they went) that too much salt would make an infant's flesh too firm

"Remarkably," the American doctor said to the mother, "you have a sodium
deficiency"

Did my mother's son feel harm before he knew the name for it?

We tell ourselves and each other stories to help us understand the what and
the why

Not all women do these things

Not all brothers do these things

When I was born, my parents put me on a rug on the ground and stood
staring at me until the light outside dimmed and then there in the
darkening we three were quiet for a while

Re
mem
ber the
handsom
e boy pla
ying ball i
n the decay
ed city? Thin
k about him
how he's pla
ying and pla
ying not as
king a singl
e question,
think abou
t that how

dreams distort a sound, since it is sent over many waters—again I cannot find my car remember where I left it, hold the key fob next to your head the waters of your mind will magnify its signal, a physicist says—even among the living it seems a dream will never end; you are dead: someone to whom things that happened will not happen again someone to whom a thing will only happen once; the house an empty socket in which an animal is enraged if given what it knows already, are you a blacksmith where you are, bending iron, love bending you, I am glad that you are dead, I am glad that you are dead, I am glad that you are glad that you are I am glad that you are I am glad that you are I am glad that dead I am dead I am dead glad that you are glad dead glad that you are dead are you dead am I dead surrendering the right to require use of any thing—even among the living this day will never end I am like a blacksmith, pushing your dark matter into the fire, I bend my

head, love attends not to me—are you a blacksmith where	you are where are you you didn't date
this dream shall I tell you what day it is this day that seem	s not to end dreams distort a sound
so how will you know my voice here's a test you can adm	inister, here's the question: the w
ord "spoiled" indicates: (a) child harmed with indulgence	(b) meat or milk gone bad (c)
soiled by spit; do not desist, do not decline to answer, m	y voice will know what to do,
do not decline, answer, do not answer, answer—push yo	u into fire you do not move but
I shake to get closer to the heat; sometimes the dead (I a	m glad that you are dead am I
glad you are dead) are buried en plein air, up there for al	l to see, to see more visible so
that others will feel that they are in a grave I am in a gra	ve I am grave am I glad you ar

the
elver
moves
as fast f-
orward a
s backwar
d; on the ro
ad he thinks
forward thin
ks back; the
young one g
rowing still
frightened
he does no
t play dead

the
elver
moves
as fast
forward a
s backwar
d; on the ro
ad he thinks
forward thin
ks back; the
young one, g
rowing still,
frightened
he does no
t play dead

An Empty House Is a Debt

1

There is a house in me. It is empty. I empty it.

Negative space: the only native emptiness there is.
There is

2

An alarm goes off. It goes on and on. When the alarm
drifts to different parts of the room,

I realize, that alarm is the sun.

3

And there is no one who does not need,

never an empty seat. And the blind one,

he does not find a place. There is a god in him
helping him to need himself.

4

A mother sticks a spoon into my chest,
which is an empty bowl, actually,

so the spoon lands quickly
and loudly. Heartbreak in the heart! she says.

5

I reach inside my empty house: as far as I'm allowed to go.
I reach outside my empty house: as far as I'm allowed to go.

6

Or don't love me, what do I care?
I am tired of feeling guilty; I am tired of running up a tab.

I want to run outside with a sack of huge penises on my back
—into the empty houses of ex-lovers, of mothers, birds
screaming out my name.

A human terrifies.
A human is someone who becomes terrified, and having become terrified,
craves an end to her fear.

This craving carves a cave.

7

What is a maze if there is nothing to find in the maze.
I find myself angry at nothing.

8

My lovers bow before me as though before Medusa.
Tell them you love them. See what they say.

Or say it to yourself, and see what you say.

When you love someone
more than you've ever known you could, it is
a good thing, except for the terrifying

realization that one day there comes
a parting.

Three

1

One evening, a man and a woman, parents to two daughters, watch *Oliver Twist* (1948), go to sleep, and in the morning, name their only son Oliver. The family rejoices (even though they are industrious refugees who previously celebrated nothing) and for several years buy him gifts, feed him sugar.

The eldest daughter resembles her brother until she wakes up one morning from a dream in which he lay in ermine, holding tightly to a scepter.

Soon after, her hips widen, one lone hair grows in her armpit. Sometimes the daughter feels like a son. Sometimes the son feels like a shadow.

"You can't draw inside the body," he says to his first grade teacher. "So why try to draw what's inside the body at all?"

2

If one has no brother, then one used to have a brother.

There is, you see, no shortage of gain and loss.

Let's admit without embellishment what we do with each other. When the daughter begins to walk, it is apparent that she ambles pigeon-toed. A doctor tells her alarmed parents that no surgery is needed, just some rollerskating. Each day after work, the father helps his daughter stay upright on her skates.

If you have a father, then you also have a son.

A child has difficulty weaning from nursing bottle to glass of milk. Concise in her expression of impatience, the mother pours a gallon of milk over the girl's head.

A tiger came across a donkey and having never seen a donkey before, mistook it for a god.

After everyone has gone to bed, an eldest child hoists her younger brother over her shoulders, then a sheet over his shoulders, and they sway as one into the middle sister's room.

Who is weak and who is weaker and what does relativity have to do with it?

3

Let me tell you a story about refugees. A mother and her dead son sit in the back seat of his car. It's intact, in their garage, and he is buckled in; she brushes the hair behind his ear. This is the old country and this is the new country and the air in the car is the checkpoint between them.

Let me tell you a story about seat belts. While driving her children to the local pool, a mother enumerates to her children their failures. *There was a mother*, she says, *who put her children in a car, sewing their seat belts so they couldn't unbuckle them, who drove them off a seaside cliff.*

A boy on a unicycle goes round and round a lighthouse, dodging tourists, ridicule, and awe. He doesn't go up, he doesn't fall down.

Son, says the mother, meaning child not her husband. Son, says the father, whose name is Son. Sister, says the son, lying in a coffin. *To hell with family*, says the rest of the family.

4

A brother is a brother when he has at least one sibling. The brother believes he is not a brother but one in name only.

When the brother meets a couple his parents' age, he takes the time to tell them he's an only child and an orphan. The three of them agree that one must not be without family, that there must be at least two in a family, that three is even better. They embrace and the couple encourages the brother, the brother waiting for the other shoe to drop. Whose shoe? His or the couple's?

Five pairs of shoes dangle from the pole of a traffic light. Over time, birds make a nest in each hollow, each separate space.

5

"Your hat is Mexican … ?" asks a sailor in Côte d'Azur.
"No, it's Moroccan."
"Are you from Japan?" asks a Moroccan shopkeeper in Marseille.
"No, I'm American."

Is belonging and fulfillment possible without family? No. Is it possible with family? No.

You cannot connect if you keep answering no.

You cannot keep your brother alive if you keep your mouth shut.

You cannot keep your brother alive.

At camp, some counselors take the kids on an excursion into the woods, leading them in a game of hide-and-seek. One boy, a deaf child who was also going blind, hid so well that they couldn't find him and he didn't find his way back. He had done everything right—

Nabokov says, "The lost glove is happy."

Is the lost brother happy?

6

A man lies in an open grave after a body is taken out of it. This practice is said to lengthen life expectancy. The brother imagines his bed is a nest in which his body is removed.

There's a story about a man galloping by another man who asks, "Where are you going?" "Ask my hearse," says the man.

"I was never lost in the jungle," says a father, "just looking for a way out."

Gyotaku

he no
w reside
s in betwe
en the sm
allest pa
rticles of
matter in our
bodies the water w
e carry in our mout
hs the dust we eat; all
provinces of Vietnam
continue to change for
m, this world is subjec
t to assembly; in my m
ind the dark sea mirr
ors the stars above,
and how I polish
it and polish it; i
t is not the body
but the self that is
a suffering form; w
aves rise and fall bu
the sea remains it do
es the same task ove
r and over again; cha
nce, discontinuity, di
scontinuity, chance; I
could have done thi
s, I could be done

he no
w reside
s in betwe
en the sm
allest pa
rticles of
matter in our
bodies the water w
e carry in our mout
hs the dust we eat; all
provinces of Vietnam
continue to change for
m, this world is subjec
t to assembly; in my m
ind the dark sea mirr
ors the stars above,
and how I polish
it and polish it; i
t is not the body
but the self that is
a suffering form; w
aves rise and fall bu
the sea remains it do
es the same task ove
r and over again; cha
nce, discontinuity, di
scontinuity, chance; I
could have done thi
s, I could be done

Time Is Filled with Beginners

Comedian on the stage, looking out at the audience before saying, "I don't
    think so" and walking off
Defy what we consider reasonable in this world
The poet says I think I can I think I can I think I can I think
Now no particular defects to speak of is good, right?
The dream about my son—or is it my mother's son—it's not about love, it's
    about loss
I rarely think about what I once was—have you ever thought about what you
    will soon become?
In Borneo, children born with six fingers are automatically treated as
    shamans, but a pianist with six fingers reports that the extra ones "just get
    in the way"
Hand perceives the finger's pain as if it were not its own
You have only to crack the egg and cradle the yolk back and forth in each
    shell until the white is gone
Weight loss mostly muscle mass atrophy too doesn't quite cut it
There's no such thing as a "correct" theory, there're "good" or "beautiful" ones,
    and like a pizza-eating contest, the one that eats the most wins
A story offers madness, mastication, masturbation and is useless when
    looked at—the characters lived happy-unhappy ever after
Tell me, please, what time it is, so I'll know I'm alive at that time

What do you say, older you?
I say I used to be.
When I smiled,
I stared at the mirror for a long time.

                                       Both of our worlds unhanded us.
I was
stranger and it was rare for a stranger
to enter town on foot at that hour, comforting herself
                      by terrifying herself,
red osiers kneeling before her as if to receive at last
the blade.

Mending in a daybreak that casts every shadow
                                except your own;
the starved fern that keeps growing,

uselessly—This is the math of it: nothing native stays.

Bitter sister, victim! I miss you.

Harps strung with gut still make music after 2,000 years.
No longer any need for ointment
in the axle. No longer any axle in the afternoon lust.

I cannot but be.
Something keeps not happening:

All the crashing waves contained inside me
        set free.

And the toast burning, like toast. Rose
                              nightgown in floral sheets. Unfinished
slice
of watermelon. A good girl knows when to lie down.

The world without me
                  is the space in this room.

                  I dress as a dog every morning
as if shaking off   a collision
                  the whip in my mouth.

The light shines brightly—

                  what new land is this?
It is not I who inhabit the suit
                but the suit that inhabits others.

I hide my real hound underground
                  give her
a man's name
       so I can hear her   howling.

         Each day I become the dog I abandon.
Nothing can stop me.

         A conduit for money
   I give alms   eat cake
      which deprives others of bread.
 I throb   from their touch
surrendering for a moment
         to the kindness of a mask
    afraid of children
        afraid of their voices, too.
At night, I whisper to my hound
        I tell her:
            when you are born
    you ride off   fall off

or steal.

The future holds good weather.

War gets everything it comes for.

Reprise

A wild dog rose, unraveling the marvel of the field.
Most fragrant hum of all shed feathers.
Like some strange music: the world started up again around him.

What if he did not depart—but we who gathered around him? Echolocation, as in the still hour before

A world is drawn, the way the—rufous bird—may find the song of a plant—poke berry, sheep sorrel—

The brine maiden's silk cascade as she moves in the night toward milk or crickets. Within captivity

We make a space we can recognize, like a root displaced from its origin, growing elsewhere, growing

Rootless and what exactly does it mean to be free, to punish the living, and what is our crime—cognac,

Loneliness, unremarkable weather? Last night before you my features darkened from adrenaline, from that

Which darkens the flesh of prey. Never have I felt guilty about anything I eat. Unaccommodating—

As they say in restaurants and relationships—for the preference of others. We who gather shift to let

Each other pass to prevent the body from abrading further. His skin against the fabric where he died /

He tore himself free / the mist dusted oaks are fixed and unseeing until someone sees them—

And in the aftermath the brother simply—flourished. The trees simply—bloomed. The field dyed massicot,

Raw chrysanthemums hammering in mist until the mist turned snow with petals. For what purpose

Do I seek love? What is the end of the world like—are we pennants in a gale murmuring amongst ourselves—

Of mere being: cilia and sinew—tell me that what we lost as collateral is also a gift.

"Empty your min
d, be formless, be
shapeless like wat
er you put water i
nto the cup, it be
comes the cup
you put water i
nto a bottle, i
t becomes the
bottle, you p
ut water into
a teapot, it b
ecomes a te
apot" it po
urs in it fl
ows out i
t drips in
to the gr
ound it
evapor
ates "b
e wate
r my
frie
nd
"

alon
g the w
ay she ga
thers smo
oth flat sto
nes, lays the
m in the yard
beside the ot
hers; her mo
saicking is slo
w her eyes s
earching for
the right sh
ape to fill t
he gap to b
ridge from
here to t
here

I thoug
ht I saw you in
the fog but it was o
nly wind Arvo Pärt's a
dagio in zero gravity, the
bows barely grazing the st
ring, the boys struggling w
ithin him like brothers free
to dwell free to—hover in
space between sound and
silence—I love from afa
r, end to end, our silho
uettes against the e
xpanse, instant
stillness

elemental thinki

ng: a   n oce
an o   f sou
nd b   etwe
en w   aters
quiv   ering
with   life,
still y   ou've
gone   about
anot   her task n   o longer between to
ne and noise—look: there are two sides to the threshold
and many ways of crossing   —we are small then we are
smaller, small, smaller, small, s   maller still we are little more tha
n matter—of the beginning of t   he end it doesn't matter, the mann
er in which we excise ourselves fill in ourselves the matter of the midd
le matters: stopped you cannot stop you cannot stop at the very end you
cannot end please let this not be th e end let me stop your end let me st
op; I acclimate to the score: I play the first part then you are silent I s
ound and silent you are part of   the whole and all around it; sma
ll, I am growing still and wi   ll fill in for you, fill you in u
ntil the end; I will nev   er give you up I will ne
ver give up   I will never

Acknowledgments

Thank you—

To my parents, Son and Khoi. To Denise, my sister. That we are together, even when apart.

To Omnidawn and Terrance Hayes, with deepest gratitude.

For their professional support: the University of Denver, Columbia University's School of the Arts, and UCLA. The 92 Street Y Unterberg Poetry Center, Academy of American Poets, Bread Loaf Writers' Conference, Bucknell University, Camargo Foundation, Catwalk Art Residency, Community of Writers at Squaw Valley, Idyllwild Arts, Key West Literary Seminars, Poetry Society of America, Provincetown Fine Arts Work Center, School of Visual Arts, and *Tin House* Summer Workshop.

To my professors, my mentors: Cal Bedient, Lucie Brock-Broido, Timothy Donnelly, Bin Ramke, Eleni Sikelianos, and Selah Saterstrom.

For their conversation and support in the editing of beta versions of this book: Gerald Maa and Rob Ostrom.

To those writing with me over the years, in biannual 15 poem-a-day intervals: Miriam Bird Greenberg, Sharif El Gammal Ortiz, Christine Shan Shan Hou, Chet'la Sebree, Elizabeth Hoover, and E.C. Belli. Emily, your heart is here beside mine.

To my fellow hungry ones: Juliana Xuan Wang, Jane Wong, Jennifer Chang, Hannah Sanghee Park, Taryn Schwilling, Alexandra Beguez, Rohan Samahon, and Genevieve Uy Gustafson. Let's eat.

To the Kileys (Jesse, Ana, and Pablo), and Jennifer Foerster, for their tenderness.

To Benjamin, the haven where most of this book was written—thank you for the unending feasts and discoveries, science and words—all my awe and love. Every day is one ripe for celebration.

Notes

In recognition of texts that have influenced the poems and what has been borrowed:

"I Keep Getting Things Wrong," stanza four is indebted to George Saunders' essay, "The Incredible Buddha Boy."

"A Necessary Death in Broad Daylight," "Family Ties," "A Woman May Not Be a Safe Place" borrows their titles from Clarice Lispector's short stories, and "Time Is Filled with Beginners" borrows its title from Lyn Hejinian. All of these poems are indebted to Lyn Hejinian's *The Unfollowing*.

"Grief Logic" is indebted to Eliot Weinberger's *An Elemental Thing*.

"A Woman May Not Be a Safe Place" takes the quote, "too much salt would make an infant's flesh too firm," from Marilynne Robinson's *Lila: A Novel*.

"An Empty House Is a Debt" is indebted to Jay Hopler's "And the Sunflower Weeps for the Sun, Its Flower."

"Ghost Of" is indebted to Richard Siken's "War of the Foxes"

"Future Self" borrows the line "Bitter sister, victim" from John Berryman's "Homage to Mistress Bradstreet."

"Reprise" borrows its form from Tessa Rumsey's *The Return Message* and is dedicated to Benjamin Finan.

"Coda" quotes Bruce Lee.

To those authors whose work I've drawn on unconsciously and am thus unable to honor here, thank you.

Born in Los Angeles, Diana Khoi Nguyen is a poet and multimedia artist whose work has appeared in *Poetry*, *American Poetry Review*, *Boston Review*, *PEN America*, and elsewhere. A winner of the 92Y Discovery / *Boston Review* Poetry Contest, she has also received awards and scholarships from the Academy of American Poets, Bread Loaf Writers Conference, and Key West Literary Seminars. She holds an MFA from Columbia University and is completing a PhD in Creative Writing at the University of Denver.

Ghost Of
by Diana Khoi Nguyen

Cover photo: "Court," from the *I'm Not There* series by Pol Ubeda

Cover and interior set in Futura Std and Minion Pro

Cover and interior design by Gillian Olivia Blythe Hamel

Printed in the United States
by Books International, Dulles, Virginia
On Glatfelter Natures Natural B19 Antique
Acid Free Archival Quality FSC Certified Recycled Paper

Publication of this book was made possible in part by gifts from:
The New Place Fund
The Clorox Company Foundation

Omnidawn Publishing
Oakland, California
2018
Rusty Morrison & Ken Keegan, senior editors & co-publishers
Trisha Peck, managing editor & program director
Gillian Olivia Blythe Hamel, senior poetry editor
Cassandra Smith, poetry editor & book designer
Sharon Zetter, poetry editor, book designer & development officer
Liza Flum, poetry editor
Avren Keating, poetry editor & fiction editor
Juliana Paslay, fiction editor
Gail Aronson, fiction editor
Tinia Montford, marketing assistant
Emily Alexander, marketing assistant
Terry A. Taplin, marketing assistant
Matthew Bowie, marketing assistant
SD Sumner, copyeditor